Q&A

A Summary of Biblical Teachings

CRC Publications
Grand Rapids, Michigan

⊛ Printed in the United States of
America on recycled paper.

Contents

Preface

This brief document, made up of eighty-four questions and answers, has been written to serve as a doctrinal basis for the "Living in Faith Everyday" (LiFE™) curriculum produced by CRC Publications in cooperation with the Reformed Church in America.* It is designed to meet the reading and comprehension level of 5th and 6th grade children. Accordingly, the concepts and language have been kept simple enough for the normal understanding of a child of that age. Since this is meant to be a "faith nurture" curriculum, the language has also been kept as personal as possible, addressing each individual child in terms of his or her own faith reaction to the biblical teachings about the way of salvation.

The order followed in this summary is the classical "sin, salvation, service" pattern of the Heidelberg Catechism. As will be evident upon reading, the main contents are also taken, often word for word, from that great confession. There are, however, additional teachings taken either from the Belgic Confession or from *Our World Belongs to God: A Contemporary Testimony*. We judged these teachings—about the Bible, covenant, kingdom, church, and the like—important for the instruction of children at this age level. These teachings were inserted in places where they seemed to fit logically; you will find them in Q&As 10-16, 21, 32, 35-38, and 65-73.

We trust and pray that this brief summary of biblical teachings according to the Reformed tradition will aid church school leaders and parents in teaching children to understand and follow the way of salvation in our Lord Jesus Christ.

Harvey A. Smit
Editor in chief
Education, Worship, and Evangelism Department

*This second (1998) edition includes several revised questions and answers.

Introduction: Our Comfort

1. What is your only comfort as a Christian?

That I,
body and soul,
in life and death,
belong to Jesus Christ.

2. What must you know to have this comfort?

First, how I sin every day
against God and my neighbor;
second, how Jesus saves me from my sin;
third, how I can show my thanks
by serving God in my daily life.

Part I: Our Sin

3. How do you know you are a sinner?

Christ's summary of the law tells me
I should love God
with all my heart, soul, and mind
and my neighbor as myself.

But I do not do this.

4. Why don't you do what God wants?

Because I naturally tend to sin,
sometimes on purpose,
sometimes without thinking.

I am like this because the first man and woman,
Adam and Eve,
chose to disobey their Creator
and became sinners.
They did this even though
they were made in God's own image,
good and obedient.

5. How sinful are you?

No part of my life is free of sin.

6. What does God think of your sin?

God hates sin and,
as the just Judge,
must punish it.

But God is also merciful
and has provided a way of salvation.

Part II: God's Salvation

7. Who can save you?

I cannot save myself.
Only Jesus Christ can save me.

8. How does Jesus save you?

As a true human being,
although without sin,
and also true God,
he was able to bear God's punishment
for the sin of all humanity.

9. Where do you learn about this salvation in Jesus Christ?

From the Bible.
It tells the story of God's saving acts
in Israel (Old Testament) and
in Jesus Christ (New Testament).

10. How do you know the Bible is true?

Because the Holy Spirit
breathed into the authors,
guiding them to write a true (infallible) account
of God's saving promises and acts.

The same Spirit told the church
which books to include in the Bible.

The same Spirit tells me,
in my heart,
that this is the true Word of God.

11. How many books are there in the Bible?

Sixty-six books;
thirty-nine in the Old Testament,
twenty-seven in the New Testament.

12. What do you read in these books?

All about God's mighty, saving acts
as told in the story of
our creation, fall, and redemption.

13. How did God bring us salvation?

Through gracious covenant promises given
to Adam and Eve in the garden,
to Noah and his family,
to Abraham and his children,
to Moses and the people of Israel,
and to all people of every nation—
whoever believes in Jesus Christ.

14. What are these covenant promises?

I will be your God,
and your children's God,
if you keep my covenant,
love me,
and serve me alone.

15. Who is included in God's covenant?

Those whom God,
according to his eternal plan and purpose,
chose out of fallen humankind
to be a separate people
in Jesus Christ.

16. How are people included in God's covenant?

By hearing the gospel of Jesus Christ,
by receiving the sign of baptism, and
by being made new (regeneration)
through the Holy Spirit's working
in their hearts and lives.

17. How does this salvation become your own?

Only by true faith
in Jesus Christ.

18. What is true faith?

True faith is a sure knowledge
of God's promises
and a firm trust
that all my sins are forgiven
for Jesus' sake.

19. What do you, as a Christian, believe?

I believe in God, the Father almighty,
creator of heaven and earth.

I believe in Jesus Christ, his only Son, our Lord,
who was conceived by the Holy Spirit
and born of the virgin Mary.
He suffered under Pontius Pilate,
was crucified, died, and was buried;
he descended to hell.
The third day he rose again from the dead.
He ascended to heaven
and is seated at the right hand
of God the Father almighty.
From there he will come to judge the living
and the dead.

I believe in the Holy Spirit,
the holy catholic church,
the communion of saints,
the forgiveness of sins,
the resurrection of the body,
and the life everlasting. Amen.

20. Does this mean you believe in three Gods: God the Father, God the Son, and God the Holy Spirit?

No.
I believe in one God,
revealed as three different persons:
Father, Son, and Holy Spirit.

21. Who is God?

God is a single, spiritual being:
eternal, invisible,
almighty, infinite,
and completely wise, just, and good.

God the Father

22. Why do you say, "I believe in God the Father almighty, creator of heaven and earth"?

Because God is
the almighty creator of heaven and earth
and the eternal Father of Jesus Christ.
God is also my faithful Father,
the one I can trust
to provide whatever I need
for body and soul.

23. What do you understand by God's providence?

That our heavenly Father
takes care of
and rules
everything in our world.

God the Son

24. Why do you say, "I believe in Jesus Christ, his only Son, our Lord"?

Because Jesus Christ,
God's eternal Son,
is my only Savior from sin.
He is my Lord
who delivers me from Satan's power
and makes me his very own.

25. What do you mean when you say, he "was conceived by the Holy Spirit and born of the virgin Mary"?

That the Holy Spirit
made the virgin Mary pregnant.
This means that her son, Jesus, is
both the eternal Son of God
and a real human being.

26. What good does this do us?

Only someone
who is truly God
and truly human
could become the go-between (mediator)
who makes us right with God.

27. What do you mean when you say, he "suffered under Pontius Pilate"?

In his life and death,
Christ suffered God's anger against sin,
shown in Pilate's judgment.
He suffered
so that we might never suffer
such severe judgment.

28. Why is it important to say, he "was crucified, died, and was buried; he descended to hell"?

Because, by hanging on the cross,
Jesus took on himself the curse of sin.
He actually died,
  and suffered the pains of hell.

He did all this to free us from eternal death.

29. What good does it do us that he "rose again from the dead"?

By rising from the dead,
Jesus
  conquered death,
  won for us a new life,
  and guaranteed our glorious resurrection.

30. What good does it do us that he "ascended to heaven and is seated at the right hand of God"?

At God's side in heaven,
Jesus
  pleads for us,
  leads his church,
  and sends his Spirit
    to pour out his gifts on us
    and defend us from all enemies.

31. How does Christ's return "to judge the living and the dead" comfort you?

I know that my Savior will come
  as the Judge.
He will condemn all his enemies
and take me
  and all his chosen ones
to the joy and glory of heaven.

32. What is our great hope?

We long for the time
when Jesus will return
  as triumphant king
to rule the universe.
Then we will live with him
  in the new creation.

God the Holy Spirit

33. What do you believe about "the Holy Spirit"?

The Holy Spirit is eternal God.

Given to me personally,
the Spirit
  makes me belong to Jesus Christ,
  comforts me,
  and stays with me forever.

34. What do you believe about "the holy catholic church" and "the communion of saints"?

The Son of God,
  through his Spirit and Word
gathers a community
  out of the entire human race.
This community is chosen
  for eternal life
  and united in true faith.

As a living member of this community,
  I must use the gifts God has given me
    to serve other members.

35. How does the Spirit help us to be true children of God?

The Spirit
  leads us in the truth,
  breaks our stubborn habits,
  and makes us obedient (sanctification).

36. How does Jesus' Spirit help the church?

The Spirit equips the church to carry out its mission:
to call disciples from all nations and
to tell everyone,
by word and deed,
the good news.

This good news is that God
in Jesus Christ
forgives our sins
and gives us new life
now and forever.

37. What do you believe about the unity of the church?

The Holy Spirit builds one church,
united in one Lord,
one faith,
one hope,
and one baptism.
This church includes believers
of every time, place, race, and language.

38. Who is head of the church?

Jesus is head of the church.

He guides and serves his church through its officers:
ministers of the Word,
evangelists,
elders, and
deacons.

39. What do you believe about "the forgiveness of sins"?

Because of Christ's sacrifice,
God pardons me from any punishment
for my sins
and for my natural tendency to sin.

40. What comfort do you find in "the resurrection of the body" and "life everlasting"?

I trust that the new life
  I now experience
will continue after death.
By Christ's power my soul and body
  will be reunited
  and made perfect.

41. What good does it do you to learn all the teachings of this creed?

No good at all
unless I truly believe in Jesus.
Only by true faith in Christ
  do I become right with God
  and receive everlasting life.

42. Why do you say that you are right with God (justified) only by faith?

Because I can't take credit
  before God
for any of the good things I do,
  not even for my own faith.

Only Christ's goodness and obedience
can make me right with God.
This becomes mine
  by God's grace
  through my faith.

43. Where does such faith come from?

The Holy Spirit creates faith in my heart
  by the gospel
and makes it sure
  by the sacraments.

The Sacraments

44. What are sacraments?

Holy signs and seals
which the Holy Spirit uses
to tell us that we are saved
by Christ's sacrifice for us on the cross.

45. How many sacraments did Christ command in the New Testament?

Two: baptism and the Lord's Supper.

46. How does baptism tell you that Christ's sacrifice is for you personally?

The water of baptism promises me
that Jesus' blood and Spirit
wash away all my sins
and make me a new person.

47. Should children of believing parents also be baptized?

Yes. By baptism,
they also are promised
that God will forgive their sin
and will send them the Holy Spirit.
They are also marked
as part of God's covenant
and of the Christian church.

48. How does the Lord's Supper tell you that Christ's sacrifice on the cross is for you personally?

I see the loaf broken
and the cup poured out
and taste the bread and wine.
This reminds me that
on the cross
Christ offered his body
and poured out his blood
for me.

49. Who may come to the Lord's table?

Those who confess their sins,
who believe Jesus died for them,
and who eagerly try
to serve and obey him.

Part III: Service

50. How should you live as a Christian?

Thankful for God's salvation,
I should live a new life
of serving Christ, my Lord,
every day in every way.

51. How do you make this new life real?

By running away from sin
and by trying eagerly to do every kind of good
as God wants me to.

52. What is this "good" God wants you to do?

Thoughts and actions which
are done out of faith,
agree with God's law,
and praise God.

53. What does God's law tell you to do?

God says in his law:

1. You shall have no other gods before me.
2. You shall not make for yourself any idols; you shall not bow down to them or worship them.
3. You shall not misuse the name of the Lord your God.
4. Remember the Sabbath day by keeping it holy.
5. Honor your father and your mother.
6. You shall not murder.
7. You shall not commit adultery.
8. You shall not steal.
9. You shall not give false testimony against your neighbor.
10. You shall not covet anything that belongs to your neighbor.

54. How are these commandments divided?

Into two tables
with four commandments in the first,
and six in the second.

The first table teaches us
what our relation to God should be.
The second table teaches us
how we should treat our neighbors.

55. What is God's will for you in the first commandment?

I should trust, love, fear, and honor
the one true God
with all my heart.
I should not trust or worship
any person, creature, or thing
in place of God.

56. What is God's will for you in the second commandment?

I should worship God only
as the Bible tells me to.

57. What is God's will for you in the third commandment?

I should never misuse or dishonor God's name;
rather, I should always use it reverently,
praising God in everything I say and do.

58. What is God's will for you in the fourth commandment?

I should regularly worship God
at Sunday church services
and do good
every day of the week.

59. What is God's will for you in the fifth commandment?

I should honor, love, and be loyal
to my father and mother
and to all others
whom God gives authority over me.

60. What is God's will for you in the sixth commandment?

I should do nothing
to insult, hurt, or kill my neighbors.
Instead I should love them
as I love myself.

61. What is God's will for you in the seventh commandment?

I should avoid all sexual sin
in thoughts, words, or actions.
I should keep myself pure and holy
in body and soul.

62. What is God's will for you in the eighth commandment?

I should not cheat or steal
from my neighbors
but do whatever I can
for their good.
I should not be greedy
but should take good care
of all God's gifts.

63. What is God's will for you in the ninth commandment?

I should not hurt my neighbor
by gossip and lying.
Instead I should love the truth
and speak it openly.

64. What is God's will for you in the tenth commandment?

With all my heart,
  I should hate sin.
I should also avoid any thought or desire
  that goes against any of God's commandments.

65. Can you obey these commandments perfectly?

Not in this life.
But they help me know
  how sinful I am,
  how much I need Christ's forgiveness,
  and how I must pray
    for the Spirit's grace
    to make me holy (sanctification).

66. What do you believe about God's kingdom?

I believe God rules
  over everyone in this world:
    both those who bow before the Lord
    and those who refuse to bow.

I believe that God's kingdom
  was promised in the Old Testament,
  came with Jesus Christ,
  and will come perfectly
    when Jesus returns.

67. What are the keys of the kingdom?

The preaching of the gospel
and Christian discipline.

These keys
  open the kingdom of heaven to believers
  and close it to unbelievers.

68. What is your responsibility as a member of God's kingdom?

To follow Jesus, my Lord,
doing his will
and trying to please him
in every part of my life.

To tell the good news
of salvation in Christ
to all people everywhere.

69. How should you think of people different from you?

No matter what our age, race, color, or sex,
we are all the human family together,
for the Creator made us all.
So I should love and respect all people.

70. How should you value human life?

Since all life is God's gift,
I should care about the well-being of others,
especially the unborn and helpless.

71. How should you think about daily work?

In all work,
even in dull tasks,
I should do my very best
so that I may honor my Lord.

72. What is your responsibility toward God's world?

God expects me
to respect all creatures,
to use nature, not to abuse it,
and to preserve the earth
in good condition
for future generations.

73. How should you think about world events?

I should trust
  that God rules and shapes
  what is happening in our world.
The future is safe,
  because our world belongs to God.

Prayer

74. Why do you need to pray?

Because prayer is the most important way
I can thank God
and because God gives good gifts
only to those who daily ask for them.

75. How should you, as a Christian, pray?

I should pray from the heart
believing that the one true God will surely
    listen to my prayer.

76. How did Jesus teach us to pray?

Our Father in heaven,
hallowed be your name,
your kingdom come,
your will be done
  on earth as it is in heaven.
Give us today our daily bread.
Forgive us our debts
  as we also have forgiven our debtors.
And lead us not into temptation,
  but deliver us from the evil one.
For yours is the kingdom
  and the power
  and the glory forever. Amen.

77. Why do we pray to God as "our Father in heaven"?

Because the almighty God is our Father
through Jesus Christ.
Our Father will give us
what we need
when we ask in faith.

78. What does "hallowed be your name" mean?

Help us to live
so that all we think, say, and do
honors and praises you.

79. What does "your kingdom come" mean?

Rule us by your Word and Spirit
so that we obey you more and more.
Keep your church strong
and add to it.
Destroy every force that fights against you
until your kingdom is complete and perfect.

80. What does "your will be done on earth as it is in heaven" mean?

Help us and all people
to obey your will
without any back talk
as willingly and faithfully
as the angels in heaven.

81. What does "give us today our daily bread" mean?

Help us trust you,
the source of everything good,
for all our daily needs.

82. What does "forgive us our debts, as we also have forgiven our debtors" mean?

For the sake of Jesus Christ,
forgive us our sins
just as we forgive our neighbors.

83. What does "lead us not into temptation, but deliver us from the evil one" mean?

Strengthen us by your Holy Spirit
so that we may fight against
the devil,
the wicked world,
and our own sinfulness.

84. Why do we end the prayer by saying, "For yours is the kingdom and the power and the glory forever. Amen"?

Because we know that you,
our all-powerful king,
will certainly hear our words
and will give us everything good.

And because your holy name
should receive all the praise, forever.